Contemporary United States

(1968 to the Present)

★★ PRESIDENTS OF THE UNITED STATES ★★

By Douglas Lynne

WEIGL PUBLISHERS INC.

Published by Weigl Publishers Inc.
350 5th Avenue, Suite 3304 PMB 6G
New York, NY 10118-0069
Website: www.weigl.com

Library of Congress Cataloging-in-Publication Data

Lynne, Douglas.
  Contemporary United States / Douglas Lynne.
     p. cm. -- (Presidents of the United States)
  Includes bibliographical references and index.
  ISBN 978-1-59036-753-7 (hard cover : alk. paper) -- ISBN 978-1-59036-754-4 (soft cover : alk. paper)
 1. Presidents--United States--Biography--Juvenile literature. 2. Presidents--United States--History--20th century--Juvenile literature. 3. Presidents--United States--History--21st century--Juvenile literature. 4. United States--History--1969---Juvenile literature. 5. United States--Politics and government--1945-1989--Juvenile literature. 6. United States--Politics and government--1989---Juvenile literature. I. Title.
  E176.1.L96 2008
  973.92092'2--dc22
  [B]

                              2007012650

Printed in the United States of America
1 2 3 4 5 6 7 8 9 0 11 10 09 08 07

Project Coordinator
Heather C. Hudak

Design
Terry Paulhus

Photo Credits
Every reasonable effort has been made to trace ownership and to obtain permission to reprint copyright material. The publishers would be pleased to have any errors or omissions brought to their attention so that they may be corrected in subsequent printings.

All of the Internet URLs given in the book were valid at the time of publication. However, due to the dynamic nature of the Internet, some addresses may have changed, or sites may have ceased to exist since publication. While the author and publisher regret any inconvenience this may cause readers, no responsibility for any such changes can be accepted by either the author or the publisher.

Contents

United States Presidents

REVOLUTION AND THE NEW NATION (1750–EARLY 1800s)

 George Washington
(1789–1797)

 John Adams
(1797–1801)

 Thomas Jefferson
(1801–1809)

 James Madison
(1809–1817)

 James Monroe
(1817–1825)

EXPANSION AND REFORM (EARLY 1800s–1861)

 John Quincy Adams
(1825–1829)

 Andrew Jackson
(1829–1837)

 Martin Van Buren
(1837–1841)

 William Henry Harrison
(1841)

 John Tyler
(1841–1845)

 James Polk
(1845–1849)

 Zachary Taylor
(1849–1850)

 Millard Fillmore
(1850–1853)

 Franklin Pierce
(1853–1857)

 James Buchanan
(1857–1861)

CIVIL WAR AND RECONSTRUCTION (1850–1877)

 Abraham Lincoln
(1861–1865)

 Andrew Johnson
(1865–1869)

 Ulysses S. Grant
(1869–1877)

DEVELOPMENT OF THE INDUSTRIAL UNITED STATES (1870–1900)

 Rutherford B. Hayes
(1877–1881)

 James Garfield
(1881)

 Chester Arthur
(1881–1885)

 Grover Cleveland
(1885–1889)
(1893–1897)

 Benjamin Harrison
(1889–1893)

 William McKinley
(1897–1901)

THE EMERGENCE OF MODERN AMERICA (1890–1930)

 Theodore Roosevelt
(1901–1909)

 William H. Taft
(1909–1913)

 Woodrow Wilson
(1913–1921)

 Warren Harding
(1921–1923)

 Calvin Coolidge
(1923–1929)

THE GREAT DEPRESSION AND WORLD WAR II (1929–1945)

 Herbert Hoover
(1929–1933)

 Franklin D. Roosevelt
(1933–1945)

POST-WAR UNITED STATES (1945–EARLY 1970s)

 Harry S. Truman
(1945–1953)

 Dwight Eisenhower
(1953–1961)

 John F. Kennedy
(1961–1963)

 Lyndon Johnson
(1963–1969)

CONTEMPORARY UNITED STATES (1968 TO THE PRESENT)

 Richard Nixon
(1969–1974)

 Gerald Ford
(1974–1977)

 Jimmy Carter
(1977–1981)

 Ronald Reagan
(1981–1989)

George H. W. Bush
(1989–1993)

 William J. Clinton
(1993–2001)

George W. Bush
(2001–)

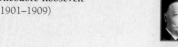

Contemporary United States

During the late 1960s and early 1970s, many people protested the United States' involvement in the Vietnam War.

As the twentieth century moved forward, the challenges faced by each new president seemed to increase. While each president's term was unique, they collectively struggled as leaders. The presidents tried to end poverty, fought wars, and dealt with national tragedies. They faced their share of scandals. Richard Nixon became the first president in U.S. history to resign from office. Ronald Reagan faced an **assassination** attempt. Bill Clinton was nearly **impeached**. Each new president, however, hoped to balance the problems of their day with the promise of a brighter tomorrow.

The era began during an ongoing struggle for power between the United States and its rival superpower, the Soviet Union. The conflict with the Soviet Union would be at the heart of many of the United States' international troubles. These two superpowers often supported opposites sides of world issues.

During the presidencies of the late 1960s to the mid-1970s, the nation was frustrated by the government's inability to resolve the Vietnam War. All across the country, young people protested U.S. involvement in the war. A civil rights movement was sweeping across the country as well. African Americans were demanding to be given equal rights. Racial tensions reached an all-time high when the leader of the movement, Dr. Martin Luther King, Jr., was assassinated in 1968.

As time wore on, the cost of the war in Vietnam was felt by the country's struggling **economy**. Through the 1970s and early 1980s, the United States suffered from the worst **inflation** and unemployment rates since the Great Depression in the 1930s. Oil-rich Arab countries imposed an embargo on oil to punish the United States for supporting Israel. The resulting energy crisis left many people distrustful of the national government and its leaders. Both Gerald Ford and Jimmy Carter worked to gain back the people's trust. They sought to find a way to stem high inflation and unemployment rates, and to ease the energy crisis.

Overseas, U.S. presidents faced many challenges. A **hostage** crisis in Iran and peace **negotiations** between Egypt and Israel were central in the late 1970s. During the 1980s, East and West Germany were unified, and the Berlin Wall was torn down, as the Cold War began to thaw. In the 1990s, the Soviet Union dissolved, and America went to war with Iraq after it had invaded Kuwait.

As the twenty-first century began, terrorism would take center stage, both in America and abroad. On September 11, 2001, terrorists attacked the United States. This attack ushered in a new focus for U.S. foreign policy, new concerns for the safety of Americans, and a new war in Iraq.

Richard Nixon's Early Years

Richard Milhous Nixon was born January 9, 1913, to a humble working-class family. His parents, Frank and Hannah Nixon, lived on a lemon farm in Yorba Linda, a town near Los Angeles, California. Frank was a temperamental man who was quick to anger. He had a keen interest in politics. Hannah was a devout **Quaker** and housewife.

Frank owned and ran a grocery store in nearby Whittier, but he struggled to make enough money to support his family. Richard spent many hours working at his father's store during high school and college to earn money to pay for his schooling.

Nixon was an excellent student who pushed himself to earn high grades. In high school, he played in the orchestra, worked on the school newspaper, and was involved in athletics. He excelled in debate, leading his school to the state championship. After high school, Nixon attended nearby Whittier College, where he was president of his class.

Nixon earned good enough grades at Whittier to receive a scholarship from the prestigious law school at Duke University in North Carolina. He knew this was a great privilege. Nixon attended Duke during the Great Depression, a time of extreme economic difficulty for the United States. Without the

Richard Nixon (standing left) enjoyed playing with his brothers Harold (middle), Arthur (right), and Donald (in the tire).

scholarship, he would not have been able to continue his schooling.

Nixon graduated from Duke in 1937. He then returned to Whittier to join a small law firm in town. It was at this time that he met his future wife, Thelma Catherine "Pat" Ryan, while auditioning for a play at the local theater. Pat Ryan was a schoolteacher with a background similar to Nixon's. On June 21, 1940, they married.

Following the Japanese attack on Pearl Harbor in 1941, the United States entered World War II. Despite his mother's Quaker beliefs, which were against participating in armed conflicts, Nixon accepted a position with a wartime government agency. He and his wife then moved to Washington, D.C. There, Nixon first learned how the federal government worked.

Nixon did not stay at his new job long, however. He wanted to enter the military and serve in the war. He enlisted in the navy as an officer and served in the Pacific. Nixon was in charge of the navy's airplanes, which flew supplies to soldiers. He did not serve in combat, but he had a successful military career, earning the rank of lieutenant commander. He left the service in 1946 after the war had ended.

In 1946, the Nixons moved back to California. The Republican Party needed a candidate to run for one of California's seats in the U.S. House of Representatives, and Nixon seemed to be the right fit. He strongly believed in

> "I believe in the American dream because I have seen it come true in my own life." *Richard Nixon*

the Republican Party's conservative views. One of the Republicans' main beliefs is that the government should have little control over people's lives and business when it comes to taxes and regulations.

Richard Nixon and his wife, Pat, welcomed their first child, Tricia, in 1946.

A Career in Politics

Following World War II, people in the United States were worried about **communism**. Communism is a form of government where the central government, not the people, owns all of a country's property and businesses. Many Americans were afraid that communist governments, such as the Soviet Union, would try to take over the world. Richard Nixon used this fear to help him win his bid for the U.S. House of Representatives. He accused his opponent, Jerry Voorhis, of being a communist. The accusation was false, but it was enough to win Nixon the election and begin his career in politics.

> "We must always remember that America is a great nation today not because of what government did for people but because of what people did for themselves and for one another." *Richard Nixon*

Communism remained a hot issue in the United States. Congress established the Un-American Activities Committee to investigate people it felt had communist ties. In his first term in office, Nixon was appointed to this committee. He helped lead a special investigation of a man named Alger Hiss. Hiss was a government worker accused of giving secret information to Whittaker Chambers, an American communist who was a spy for the Soviet Union. Hiss claimed he was innocent and did not know Chambers. Nixon worked hard to prove Hiss was lying.

The tide turned in Nixon's favor when Chambers led officials to stolen documents he had hidden inside a pumpkin in his garden. These "pumpkin papers" tied Hiss to Chambers, and Hiss was sent to prison. The investigation and conviction of Hiss made Nixon a household name.

Richard Nixon (seated, center) gained fame as a member of the Un-American Activities Committee during the trial of Alger Hiss.

Serving as vice president to Dwight Eisenhower, Richard Nixon prepared for his future as president.

The Republican Party saw Nixon as a political fighter and asked him to run for a seat in the U.S. Senate. Again, Nixon attacked his opponent, Helen Gahagan Douglas, as sympathizing with communists. He caught her off guard with his **campaign** tactics and again took the seat despite her popularity. At age 38, Nixon became the youngest member of the Senate.

The Republican Party had bigger plans for Nixon, however. Dwight Eisenhower was chosen as the Republican candidate for the 1952 presidential election. Nixon was asked to be his running mate.

Eisenhower was respected because of his military service in World War II. He was older than Nixon, quiet, and reserved. He refused to say anything bad about his opponent, Adlai Stevenson. The Republicans looked to Nixon, who appeared willing to do anything to win, to attack Stevenson. Together, Eisenhower and Nixon went on to win the 1952 and 1956 elections.

Nixon played an active role in helping Eisenhower run the country. He assumed the president's duties three times when Eisenhower faced health problems. He would be one of the most active vice presidents of all time and make the role of vice president more important in the U.S. government.

CHECKERS SPEECH

During the 1952 presidential campaign, Nixon was accused of accepting a large amount of money while he was a senator and then using the money for personal expenses. Many Republicans feared the scandal would hurt Eisenhower in the election, and they encouraged him to remove Nixon from the Republican ticket.

To prove his innocence, Nixon addressed the American public in a speech, which became known as the "Checkers" speech. Nixon admitted he had accepted the money but said that he never used it inappropriately. The funds were only used for political expenses. The speech earned its name because Nixon admitted his family had kept one gift, a small cocker spaniel named Checkers. Eisenhower stood by his running mate, and together they went on to win the election.

Nixon's Presidency

Despite Nixon's successful terms as vice president, his success in the political arena was far from guaranteed. In 1960, he faced Democrat John F. Kennedy in the presidential race and lost. Nixon then headed back to California. He worked as a lawyer but missed political life. In 1962, Nixon ran for governor of California. He lost this election and feared his political career was over.

Following the assassination of President Kennedy in 1963, Lyndon Johnson took office. Johnson escalated the Vietnam War. At first, the United States only sent military advisors to help South Vietnam. Later, U.S. troops were sent to protect South Vietnam from North Vietnam. Johnson's failure to win the war was one reason he chose not to run for re-election in 1968.

The Republican Party again looked to Nixon to run for president. During the campaign, Nixon promised to fight crime and inflation. He vowed to bring back order to the country, which had seen civil rights and anti-war protests turn violent. He said he would seek an honorable way for America to end the Vietnam War. Nixon defeated Democratic candidate Hubert Humphrey in the 1968 election.

Nixon's first task was to deal with the Vietnam crisis. He reduced the number of troops in Vietnam. He ordered bombings in Cambodia and Laos to cut off North Vietnam's supply routes. These attacks led to more protests at home, but eventually, peace talks with North Vietnam succeeded. The last U.S. troops left Vietnam in 1973.

The presidential debate between Richard Nixon and John F. Kennedy was the first to be televised. Nixon appeared nervous, and it hurt his chances in the election.

After the war, Nixon realized he needed to improve U.S. foreign relations. He began with China and the Soviet Union. They had been allies with North Vietnam. Nixon's visit to China led the two countries to have full-diplomatic relationships for the first time in nearly 25 years. In 1972, Nixon became the first U.S. president to visit the Soviet Union. He and Soviet leader Leonid Brezhnev signed the Strategic Arms Limitation Treaty. They agreed to limit the manufacture of nuclear weapons.

Nixon worked hard at home as well. He supported NASA, and the United States became the first country to land a human on the Moon. Nixon established the Environmental Protection Agency to monitor and control pollution and the Drug Enforcement Agency to enforce federal drug laws.

Richard Nixon met with Chinese leader Chairman Mao Zedong on Nixon's historic trip to China in 1972.

Nixon won re-election in 1972. Soon, however, Nixon's good fortunes soured. Vice President Spiro Agnew resigned after being accused of tax evasion and bribery. Nixon replaced Agnew with Gerald Ford. Then, Nixon and several of his top advisors were connected to an attempted break-in of the Democratic National Party Headquarters in the Watergate Hotel.

"The greatest honor history can bestow is the title of peacemaker. This honor now beckons America."
Richard Nixon

As the matter was investigated, Nixon realized his part in the scandal would be revealed. To avoid a trial and possible impeachment, he did something that no other president in U.S. history had done before him. Nixon resigned from office. He announced his resignation in a television address to the nation on August 8, 1974. Nearly 20 years later, on April 22, 1994, Nixon passed away. He was 81 years old.

Watergate

During Nixon's run for re-election, campaign tactics took a turn for the worse. The Committee to Re-elect the President (CREEP) used illegal gifts of money to try to discover what the Democrats were planning. They even broke into Democratic Party National Headquarters at the Watergate Hotel in Washington, D.C., in June 1972.

A group of Nixon's trusted advisors had hired five men to break into the office in the hopes that they would find information to use against the Democrats. The men were told to place listening devices on the telephones in hopes of learning the plans for the Democratic Party's campaign. CREEP's plans backfired, however, when the burglars were caught.

At first, the incident received little attention. Within days, Nixon had decided to end the investigation into the burglary. He knew that if investigators looked too closely into the incident, they would uncover other illegal activities. Nixon tried to cover up his involvement, but the American public began to distrust him. They began to realize that even though he may not have committed the crimes, he had to have known about them.

> "To have served in this office is to have felt a very personal sense of kinship with each and every American. In leaving it, I do so with this prayer: May God's grace be with you in all the days ahead."
>
> *Richard Nixon, resignation speech*

John D. Ehrlichman, one of Nixon's officials, was met by media outside a Washington, D.C., courthouse after being sentenced for his role in the Watergate Scandal.

The scandal grew larger when the U.S. Senate decided to launch an investigation. The events being investigated became known as the Watergate Scandal. Even though Nixon convinced his aides to lie for him, news came out that Nixon routinely made audiotapes of the conversations that took place in the oval office. Senate investigators asked Nixon to give them the tapes, but he refused. At first he said it was because many of the conversations were of a sensitive nature and could hurt the U.S. government if they were released. He was actually worried that the tapes would reveal his role in the Watergate Scandal.

The committee demanded the tapes, and Nixon decided to compromise. He gave the commission a written transcript of the tapes, but some of the information had been removed. Finally, the U.S. Supreme Court ordered Nixon to turn over the tapes. This was disastrous for Nixon. Not only did the tapes reveal that he had known about the burglary, they proved that he had tried to cover it up.

When Congress realized that Nixon had tried to hide the illegal activities that had occurred, he lost the last support he had. Nixon knew that if he were forced to stand trial, he would be found guilty and face impeachment. He decided to resign from office effective August 9, 1974. He became the first president to do so. Vice President Gerald Ford then assumed the role of president. Shortly after his **inauguration**, President Ford pardoned Nixon of all of his crimes to help the country heal and move on.

Richard Nixon gave his staff the "thumbs up" sign as he said goodbye after resigning.

Gerald Ford's Early Years

Gerald R. Ford, Jr., was born Leslie Lynch King, Jr., on July 14, 1913, in Omaha, Nebraska. He was originally named after his biological father, who was an unkind husband. Gerald's mother, Dorothy Gardner King, left her husband two weeks after Gerald was born. She moved to Grand Rapids, Michigan, to live with her parents. Dorothy divorced Gerald's father and made a new life on her own with her young son, whom she called "Junie." Later, she met and married the man that Gerald came to call "Dad," Gerald R. Ford. Gerald did not find out about his real father until he was in high school. In 1935, he legally changed his name to Gerald Rudolf Ford, Jr., as a sign of respect for the man who raised him.

"Truth is the glue that holds government together. Compromise is the oil that makes governments go."
Gerald Ford

Ford was an outstanding athlete and an excellent student. His skill on the field helped earn him spots on the All-City and All-State football teams. He was very active in scouting, eventually earning the highest rank of Eagle Scout.

Ford did not have enough money to attend college, but his grades and athletic skill earned him a scholarship to the University of Michigan between 1931 and 1935. Again, he excelled, leading the Wolverines football team to two national titles. Following graduation, Ford received offers to play professional football from the Detroit Lions and the Green Bay Packers. He turned them both down to attend Yale University to study law.

Young Gerald Ford (left) had three half-brothers—Tom (pictured), Richard, and James.

Since money was still a problem, Ford took a job coaching football and boxing at Yale. After earning his law degree in 1941, he returned to Grand Rapids to set up a law practice. He taught at the university there and became an active member of the local Republican Party.

Ford's law career was put on hold when the United States entered World War II. Ford enlisted in the navy. He was assigned to the U.S.S. *Monterey*, an aircraft carrier. The *Monterey* would see a great deal of combat during the war.

The greatest opponent the *Monterey's* crew faced was the "Great Typhoon." It was one of the worst storms ever to be recorded in the Pacific Ocean. Ford almost fell to his death when he lost his footing as huge waves washed over the ship's rails.

Ford left the navy in 1946. He then returned to Grand Rapids and took a job with one of the best law firms in town. Ford established himself as an honest, hardworking employee. He seemed to possess a natural talent for earning people's trust.

It was at this time that Ford was introduced to his future wife, Betty Bloomer Warren. A former dancer and model, Betty had a successful career in fashion at one of the large department stores in town. Ford and Betty got along well, and it did not take long for them to realize that they belonged together. On October 15, 1948, they were married. One month later, Ford won his first political election.

Ford and a former school classmate made a plan to win the Republican **nomination** for the U.S. House of Representatives away from longtime **incumbent** Bartel Jonkman. They waited until the last minute to enter the race so as to surprise their opponent. The plan worked. Ford won the nomination and went on to win the election easily.

Gerald R. Ford (right) served in the U.S. Navy during World War II.

Ford's Presidency

Ford established himself early in his political career as someone who made up his own mind about issues. He was a moderate when it came to foreign affairs, supporting President Truman's Point Four program, which aimed to help underdeveloped countries by providing technological skills, knowledge, and equipment. He was more conservative on domestic issues, believing in lower taxes and fewer government regulations. Ford's natural ability to work with people allowed him to stand his ground without making political enemies. One of his first friends in Washington, D.C., was Richard Nixon.

> "My fellow Americans, our long national nightmare is over."
> *Gerald Ford*

The people of Michigan re-elected Ford 12 times to the U.S. House of Representatives. Over his years as a Congressman, Ford was part of many important committees. In 1965, he became house minority leader. During this time, President Lyndon Johnson appointed Ford to the Warren Commission, which was a special task force assembled to investigate the assassination of President John F. Kennedy. In this role, Ford supported the idea that only one assassin, Lee Harvey Oswald, took part in Kennedy's death.

Ford maintained excellent relationships with his fellow politicians. As a result, he was the perfect candidate to replace Vice President Spiro Agnew, who had resigned because of a bribery scandal. One year later, in 1974, Nixon's resignation made Ford the 38th president.

President Ford entered office at a difficult time. Following the Watergate Scandal, trust in the government was at an all-time low. Inflation and unemployment plagued the nation. Oil and gas were in short supply. Ford was a Republican president who had to deal with a mostly Democratic Congress. All his efforts would be a struggle.

Gerald Ford was the house minority leader until becoming vice president in 1973.

Ford's first major decision was one that would haunt him throughout his term in office. He decided to put an end to the Watergate Scandal. He felt that pardoning Nixon of his crimes would allow the country to move forward and heal. It was an unpopular decision.

Still, Ford moved forward. On the home front, he worked out a compromise in Congress to lower inflation and unemployment rates and signed a bill that established special education for handicapped children. Internationally, he traveled to continue the goodwill Nixon had started. Ford also was part of the Helsinki Agreement in which 35 countries came together to establish human rights regulations.

Despite all his efforts, Ford nearly lost the Republican nomination to Ronald Reagan for the 1976 election. Ford ran against Democrat Jimmy Carter and lost in one of the closest presidential races in U.S. history.

After the defeat, Ford and Betty retired to their home in California. There, Ford wrote his autobiography. He toured the country and spoke to students about how the U.S. government works. In 1999, Ford received the Presidential Medal of Freedom, the highest honor a citizen can receive. President Clinton gave him this award for his role in restoring peace and trust to the country following the Watergate Scandal. Ford also earned the Congressional Gold Medal from Congress.

For a man who had never sought the position of president, Ford managed to make a positive impact on the country during the two-and-a-half years he served. Ford died December 26, 2006. He was 93 years old.

People showed their anger and distrust in the government after President Ford pardoned Nixon.

NIXON PARDON

When Ford took over as president, Americans distrusted the government more than ever before. Ford knew he needed to help the country move forward and to rebuild Americans' trust. He knew Congress could not deal with important issues with the Watergate Scandal looming overhead. Ford wanted to put a quick end to the whole ugly affair.

Many people were shocked and angry at Ford's decision to pardon Nixon. Some felt he had made a secret deal with Nixon. Nixon would resign from office so that Ford could become president, but only if Ford would then pardon him. In the end, Ford's decision cost him the 1976 election.

Jimmy Carter's Early Years

> "We become not a melting pot but a beautiful mosaic. Different people, different beliefs, different yearnings, different hopes, different dreams." *Jimmy Carter*

James Earl Carter, Jr., was born in Plains, Georgia, on October 1, 1924. His parents, Earl and Lillian, were peanut farmers who instilled a strong work ethic and a deep Baptist faith in James, also known as "Jimmy." His father's involvement in politics helped shape his life. Jimmy and his dad traveled to nearby political barbeques where they would listen to politicians giving speeches. His parents encouraged him to learn about the government.

Jimmy's mother taught him to be open-minded. She taught him about civil rights and to care for those less fortunate. Growing up in the deep South, one the biggest issues of the day was **segregation**. Many southerners felt that African Americans and people of European ancestry should be kept apart. Jimmy's mother felt strongly that all people deserved the same rights. She taught her children to stand up for their beliefs and to respect people of all races.

Carter excelled in school. He belonged to the Future Farmers of America, which teaches students leadership and career skills through agricultural education. Carter wanted to do more than farm, though. He wanted to go to college and see the world. He attended the U.S. Naval Academy and graduated in 1946 with a degree in

Like his parents, Jimmy Carter was a peanut farmer in Georgia.

engineering. His hope was to one day command a submarine. It was at this time that Carter married a woman from his hometown, Rosalynn Smith.

Carter began his career in the navy as an engineer aboard submarines. It was a challenging life. After seven years of service, Carter learned that his father was dying of cancer. He packed up his family and moved them back home to Plains so he could help run the family farm.

In short order, Carter and Rosalynn improved the way the farm and family business were run. Carter soon became actively involved in the community, landing a position on the local school board. He hoped to end segregation in the schools. He wanted to make sure that African American children received the same educational advantages as other children.

In 1962, Carter felt that the time was right to run for political office. He entered the race for a seat in the Georgia state senate. He wanted to take a greater role in solving his state's educational issues. Carter won the election, and his political career began. He moved the family to Atlanta, the state capital.

Soon, Carter was seeking higher office. He ran for governor in 1966. He lost but ran again in 1970 and won. As governor, he worked to end racial discrimination, spoke about the environment, and sought to make the government more efficient.

Carter eventually received recognition from the Democratic Party, and they chose him to be their candidate in the 1976 presidential election. Carter selected

Minnesota Senator Walter Mondale to be his running mate. His platform during the election centered on human rights. Carter said that Americans were lucky to live in a **democracy** where their basic human freedoms are guaranteed. He ran against Republican President Gerald Ford, who was seeking re-election. It was one of the closest races in history. Carter received 50 percent of the popular vote and won 297 electoral votes. Ford received 48 percent of the popular vote, winning 240 electoral votes.

Rosalynn Smith Carter played an important role in her husband's successful campaigns for governor and president.

Carter's Presidency

When Jimmy Carter took office, there were many problems facing the country, and the public's expectations that Carter could fix things were very high. Carter entered office with inflation and unemployment at all-time highs. The country slipped into a recession, a time when the economy slows down. High gas prices caused an energy crisis, which made the economy worse. Carter urged Americans to conserve energy, and he set money aside to search for alternative forms of energy.

> "Let us create together a new national spirit of unity and trust."
> *Jimmy Carter*

Carter achieved great things through his efforts. He created the Department of Energy to deal with the energy crisis. This organization helped the country use its energy more efficiently. Carter worked hard to protect the environment. He signed the Alaska National Interests Lands Conservation Act, which set aside more than 100 million acres of land to be turned into national parks. Carter knew education was the way to a bright future, so he created the Department of Education to improve schools across the country.

Carter had an impact on foreign affairs. In 1978, he organized a summit between the leaders of Egypt and Israel. These countries were at odds with each other, and Carter arranged a peace treaty between them as well as a plan for peace in the Middle East. He established working relations with the Chinese government, and he negotiated the SALT II Treaty with the Soviet Union to further reduce the number of nuclear weapons each country would

Jimmy Carter chose Minnesota Senator Walter Mondale as his running mate in the 1976 election.

produce. Carter worked on a treaty to transfer U.S. control of the Panama Canal back to Panama.

In 1979, Carter faced several setbacks. The Soviet Union invaded Afghanistan. Carter knew he had to take a strong stand to show America's disapproval. The Soviet Union relied on the United States for much of its grain. Carter enacted a grain embargo, refusing to supply the needed grain. He made the difficult decision to withdraw from the Moscow Olympics. He decided he could not support the Soviet Union in any way. Carter's decisions had adverse effects in America, however. The grain embargo hurt American farmers, and the boycott of the Olympics took the chance to compete away from many athletes. It was a tough blow, but not the worst to come.

That same year, a group of Iranian students stormed into the American Embassy in Tehran to protest Carter's assistance to the exiled Shah of Iran. This ex-leader of Iran was in the United States seeking medical treatment. The students ultimately held 52 U.S. hostages and demanded that the United States return the Shah so he could be put on trial.

Carter was unable to negotiate with the terrorists. Instead, he approved a plan to try to rescue the hostages. The rescue mission failed when three helicopters malfunctioned. Despite the fact that the Shah died months later in Egypt, the Iranians did not release the hostages. They were held for a total of 444 days.

The hostage crisis was one reason Carter lost his re-election bid in 1980. The hostages were released the same day Carter left office.

Today, Carter continues his fight for human rights. In 1999, he was awarded the Presidential Medal of Freedom. In 2002, he became the third president to receive the Nobel Peace Prize. He is currently the oldest living ex-president.

CAMP DAVID ACCORDS

Jewish immigrants had fled to Palestine because of World War II. Tensions rose in the Middle East as Palestinians were displaced by the immigrants. The United Nations hoped to solve the problem by creating Jewish and Arab regions in Palestine. By 1948, the Jewish region wanted to become the independent state of Israel. Palestinians and nearby Muslim countries refused to accept Israel.

When Carter became president, settling the conflict between Israel and its neighbors was his top priority. In 1978, he invited Egypt's president, Anwar al-Sadat, and Israel's prime minister, Menachem Begin, to the presidential retreat at Camp David. For 13 days, the three negotiated. In the end, they developed a trust and friendship that resulted in a historic peace treaty. Egypt became the first Muslim country to recognize Israel as an independent state. Sadat and Begin were awarded the Nobel Peace Prize later that year.

Ronald Reagan's Early Years

Ronald Wilson Reagan was born February 6, 1911, in the small town of Tampico, Illinois. His family was poor, but he had a happy childhood. His parents, Nellie and Jack, nicknamed Ronald "Dutch."

Ronald attended high school in Dixon, where he played football and acted in plays. He was an excellent student. Ronald spent summers working as a lifeguard at a local park. He is credited with saving many lives and was a local hero. Ronald later attended Eureka College, where he worked on the school newspaper, was student council president, and graduated with degrees in economics and sociology.

Reagan's first career was in acting. He landed a job at a radio station in Iowa announcing sporting events. Soon, his communication skills would lead to a big break. While working at a baseball spring training event, Reagan met a Hollywood movie agent. His good looks and personality won him an audition for a movie role. He so impressed the studio executives that within a few days he received a movie contract from Warner Brothers. Just like that, he was on his way to Hollywood. He earned $200 a week making movies. Reagan met Jane Wyman, a fellow actor, and the two married on January 26, 1940.

When the United States entered World War II, Reagan felt the call to enlist in the Air Force. His poor eyesight prevented him from becoming a pilot, so he made flight-training films for the army. The acting skills he had honed in Hollywood were put to good use.

Ronald Reagan (middle right) grew up in Illinois with his parents, Jack and Nelle, and his older brother, Neil (middle left).

Following the war, Reagan turned his attention to improving working conditions and gaining rights for actors. In 1947, he became president of the Screen Actors Guild (SAG). Reagan's work for this organization led him to Washington, D.C., where he developed an interest in politics.

After his divorce from Jane Wyman, Reagan met and married another actress, Nancy Davis. In his time as an actor, Reagan made 53 movies. He is best remembered for his role in the movie *Knute Rockne - All American*. He was also successful in television, appearing on such shows as *General Electric Theater* and *Death Valley Days*.

Reagan's first entry into politics was to help others in their campaigns. He became a leader in California's Republican Party and toured the country speaking on the party's behalf. He helped politicians raise money for their campaigns. In 1964, Reagan taped a speech called "A Time for Choosing," in which he called the American public to action. In it, he said, "You and I have a rendezvous with destiny." He was well on his way to gaining the skills that would make him known as "The Great Communicator." Reagan quickly gained respect in the Republican Party, and by 1966, they asked him to run for governor of California.

Ronald Reagan earned fame as an actor, performing in movies such as *International Squadron*.

Reagan's Early Political Career

> "They say the world has become too complex for simple answers. They are wrong. There are no easy answers, but there are simple answers. We must have the courage to do what we know is morally right."
>
> *Ronald Reagan*

Ronald Reagan was one of the first politicians to successfully use television to campaign. His opponent, incumbent Governor Edmund Brown, did not take Reagan seriously because of his acting career. Reagan's charm, good looks, and TV appearances helped get people to listen to his ideas. He won the election, as well as his re-election in 1970. His supporters felt Reagan could go far in politics and encouraged him to run for president.

By 1976, Reagan felt confident that he had the skills necessary to run the country. He decided to take on President Gerald Ford for the Republican presidential nomination. He lost, and at 65 years old, many people thought Reagan was too old to run the country.

Reagan persevered. He continued to study politics and history, and decided he wanted to make one last run for the presidency. In 1980, he battled George H.W. Bush for the Republican nomination and eventually took him as his running mate. With inflation and unemployment plaguing the country, Carter was an easy target during the campaign. Carter was receiving a great deal of criticism concerning the Iranian hostage crisis.

Governor Ronald Reagan addressed the Republican National Convention in 1968.

George H.W. Bush (right) served as Ronald Reagan's vice president for eight years before becoming president himself.

Reagan criticized Carter's policies, both at home and abroad. He told the American public he hoped to improve the economy, strengthen the military, and balance the budget.

Together, Reagan and Bush were a good team, and the tides turned in their favor when hostage negotiations fell apart for Carter. Reagan went on to win the presidency in an overwhelming victory, winning 489 electoral votes to Carter's 49. When he took office, Reagan was just three weeks shy of his 70th birthday and the oldest president ever elected.

Reagan's first act as president was to welcome home the hostages. The Iranians, angry with Carter for failing to give them what they wanted, waited until he left office to release the hostages. Reagan is often given credit for negotiating their release. Reagan's first term in office had a rocky start, as there was an attempt on his life. His good humor and grace during the crisis caused his popularity to soar.

ASSASSINATION ATTEMPT

Most presidents have to face difficult challenges during their terms in office. Few, however, face an assassination attempt and survive. Just nine weeks after his inauguration in 1981, President Reagan was seriously wounded by a gunshot fired by John Hinckley outside a Washington, D.C., hotel. He was rushed to nearby George Washington University Hospital.

Doctors removed a bullet that had entered Reagan's lung and lodged itself less than an inch from his heart. Despite the pain, Reagan managed to retain his sense of humor. He even said to the surgeons who would be operating on him, "I hope you're all Republicans!"

Reagan was quick to recover from his wounds. Less than a month later, he addressed Congress with his economic plan for the country.

Reagan's Presidency

Ronald Reagan's first course of action was to strengthen the economy. He initiated legislation that would stop inflation, increase the employment rate, and strengthen U.S. defenses. Reagan's approach to economics would come to be known as "Reaganomics." His plan called for the federal government to spend less, which would lower the taxes people paid. People would then have more money to spend. That would strengthen businesses and, in turn, strengthen the economy.

Reagan continued to cut taxes but increased government spending, especially in the area of defense. The federal **deficit** rose to record highs. Americans accepted the deficit, however, because the country was enjoying its longest period without a recession or depression.

During Reagan's first term in office, tensions increased around the world. With the Cold War raging, Reagan stockpiled nuclear weapons as a show of strength. This sparked an arms race with the Soviet Union.

Reagan sent troops into Beirut, Lebanon, as part of an international peacekeeping effort. The Americans' presence in the area was not popular with the people of Lebanon. In 1983, a terrorist attack at a U.S. military base in Beirut left 241 marines dead. Reagan also faced challenges in other parts of the world. Just two days after the attack in Beirut, he sent troops to Grenada, an island in the Caribbean. The government

President Ronald Reagan waved to a crowd in Washington, D.C., shortly before the assassination attempt on his life.

President Reagan met with Soviet leader Mikhail Gorbachev to discuss an arms treaty in 1986.

of Cuba wanted to take over the island to establish a communist government there. The U.S. invasion served to protect American students in Grenada and to stop the spread of communism.

Reagan retained his popularity, easily winning re-election in 1984. He continued to take a strong stand in his second term and again faced terrorists. Reagan accused Libyan leader Muammar al-Qaddafi of sponsoring terrorism around the world. In 1986, a terrorist attack in Germany killed an American serviceman and injured many others. Reagan thought Qaddafi was connected to this attack. He responded by bombing Tripoli, Libya, and striking Qaddafi's home.

Reagan faced other issues. Doctors discovered cancer in his large intestine. His recovery was a success, but tragedy lay elsewhere. In January 1986, NASA prepared to send the first non-astronaut into space, a teacher named Christa McAuliffe. As the world watched, the Space Shuttle Challenger exploded just after takeoff, killing everyone on board.

When the country's mood was at an all-time low, Reagan improved relations with the Soviet Union. He met several times with Mikhail Gorbachev, the leader of the Soviet Union. They signed a treaty to reduce the number of nuclear missiles each country had. This event was a sign of things to come. The Cold War was thawing, and the Soviet Union's power was weakening. Some people believed it was because the Soviet Union could not keep up in the arms race that Reagan began.

After his second term in office, Reagan retired to California. Shortly afterward, he was diagnosed with Alzheimer's disease. He retreated from public view, and after 10 years of living with the illness, Reagan died on June 5, 2004. He was 93 years old.

"What I'd really like to do is go down in history as the president who made Americans believe in themselves again." *Ronald Reagan*

George H.W. Bush's Early Years

George Herbert Walker Bush was born June 12, 1924. He was born in Milton, Massachusetts, but grew up in Greenwich, Connecticut. Prescott, George's father, was a wealthy businessman and a U.S. Senator. He imparted his ideas about "duty, service, and discipline" to all of his children. Dorothy, George's mother, instilled good manners, respect, and sportsmanship in her son.

George attended a private boarding school in Andover. He was an excellent student and became an accomplished athlete. Shortly after his high school graduation in 1942, he met the woman who would later become his wife, Barbara Pierce.

Bush enlisted in the U.S. Navy on his 18th birthday. He was trained

as a pilot and assigned duty aboard the aircraft carrier *San Jacinto* during World War II. His main job was to fly information-gathering missions, photographing possible locations where the enemy may have stored weapons. While on one of these missions, Bush almost lost his life. His plane crashed into the Pacific. He was rescued by a submarine and received the Distinguished Flying Cross for his bravery during the mission.

In World War II, George H.W. Bush flew a three-man Grumman Avenger torpedo-bomber plane.

Bush returned home and married Barbara on January 6, 1945. The two settled in Virginia Beach, Virginia, where George spent the rest of his naval career training pilots. After leaving the military, he furthered his education by attending Yale University in New Haven, Connecticut. During his first year there, he and Barbara had their first son, George Walker Bush, Jr., who would grow up to be the 43rd president of the United States The Bushes had five more children.

Bush excelled in school while maintaining a family. He became the captain of the baseball team and played in the first College World Series in 1947. Yale lost to the University of California at Berkeley. Bush graduated with a degree in economics. Instead of working in the family business, he and Barbara headed to Texas to make a name for

themselves in the oil business. His good instincts soon made him a successful businessman and a self-made millionaire.

Bush's energies turned toward politics. Texas was mainly a Democratic state, and the Bush family had a long history with the Republican Party. As a result, Bush lost his first attempt at a U.S. Senate seat in 1964. Undeterred, he sold his business and dedicated himself to a political career, earning respect in Texas and a seat in the U.S. House of Representatives in 1966 and again in 1968.

> "The United States is the best and fairest and most decent nation on the face of the earth."
>
> *George H.W. Bush*

Prescott Bush's life as a senator inspired George to follow a career in politics.

Bush's Political Career

Bush's background in business and economics made him a strong leader. He was assigned to the Ways and Means Committee, which helps determine how the government spends its money. Throughout the 1970s, he served as ambassador to the United Nations, head of the Republican National Committee, head of the U.S. liaison office in China, and finally as director of the Central Intelligence Agency.

In 1980, Bush decided to run for president. He fell short of receiving the Republican nomination, but he joined Ronald Reagan as his vice presidential candidate. The two developed a good partnership and served in the White House together from 1981 to 1989.

Bush took an active role as vice president, seeking alternative energy sources, visiting foreign countries, and helping deal with the growing problem of illegal drug trade and smuggling. Finally, Bush decided to make another run for president in the 1988 election. He ran against Democrat Michael Dukakis, the governor of Massachusetts. After promising not to raise taxes, Bush won the election. He entered his presidency facing the largest federal deficit in American history. He eventually was forced to break his campaign promise in order to stabilize the deficit.

Bush's experience as a statesman helped him with foreign affairs. He sent troops into Panama to help capture General Manuel Noriega, the leader of a corrupt government that trafficked in drugs. Bush worked with Soviet leader Mikhail Gorbachev to sign the first Strategic Arms Reduction Treaty to reduce nuclear arms. He helped bring along the end of the Cold War as the Soviet Union ceased to exist. This once great power broke apart into Russia and several smaller countries.

George H.W. Bush campaigned in Mississippi for his 1988 presidential bid.

Bush's greatest test was yet to come. In 1990, Iraqi President Saddam Hussein invaded the small Middle Eastern country of Kuwait in his attempt to control the world's oil supply. With the backing of the United Nations, U.S. forces successfully defeated Saddam's army and freed Kuwait.

Another one of Bush's achievements was the signing of the North American Free Trade Agreement with Mexico and Canada. Bush hoped this agreement would encourage more trade between the countries of North America.

Bush felt confident that, with his successes, he would win re-election in 1992. However, high crime rates and a faltering economy cost him the presidency.

The Bushes returned to their home in Houston and continued to work in public service. Together, Bush and Barbara have visited many foreign countries and welcomed visitors from other countries to the United States. They watched as two of their sons achieved success in politics. Jeb became governor of Florida, and George became governor of Texas, and later, the president of the United States.

"America is never wholly herself unless she is engaged in high moral principle. We as a people have such a purpose today. It is to make kinder the face of the nation and gentler the face of the world."
George H.W. Bush

U.S. soldiers based in Saudi Arabia helped free Kuwait from Iraqi occupation.

OPERATION DESERT STORM

Iraqi leader Saddam Hussein wanted to control the oil supply in the Middle East. His plan included invasions into the oil-rich countries of Kuwait and Saudi Arabia, his neighbors in the Middle East. Bush reacted quickly and forcefully when Iraq invaded Kuwait in 1990. He joined forces with a **coalition** from 30 different countries. With the full support of Congress, Bush gave Hussein a deadline—leave Kuwait by January 15, 1991, or be prepared to go to war.

When the deadline arrived and Saddam still refused to remove his troops, U.S. forces led the allied forces in land and air attacks against Iraq. They entered Kuwait, and in just six weeks, forced the Iraqis out and defeated Hussein. The organized attack against Iraq became known as "Operation Desert Storm."

William J. Clinton's Early Years

William Jefferson Blyth was born on August 19, 1946, in Hope, Arkansas. He would never know his biological father, who was killed in an automobile accident before he was born. Years later, his mother, Virginia, married Roger Clinton. William took his stepfather's last name when he was 15 years old. He eventually became known as Bill Clinton.

The family moved to Hot Springs, Arkansas. Life was hard, but despite problems with his stepfather, Bill became a popular student who excelled in both academics and music. He loved to play the saxophone and even started a jazz band named The Three Blind Mice. Bill considered a career in music until he attended Boys' Nation, a program in which high school students learn about the workings of the U.S. government in Washington, D.C. There, Bill had a chance meeting with President John F. Kennedy, which caused him to change his focus. Bill decided that he, too, wanted to make an impact on the world, like President Kennedy.

Clinton attended Georgetown University in Washington, D.C., and he thrived in the nation's capital. He spent his summers working on local campaigns and became an aide to Senator J. William Fulbright of Arkansas. In 1968, Clinton won a Rhodes scholarship, which allowed him to spend the next two years studying at Oxford University in Great Britain. Upon his return, Clinton enrolled in the Yale School of Law. There, he met the kind of people who could help him in the future as a politician. He met a fellow law student named Hillary Rodham. She, too, wanted to do great things for her country. They became fast friends. After graduation, Clinton returned to Arkansas to teach law at the University of Arkansas.

In 1963, young Bill Clinton met President John F. Kennedy in Washington, D.C.

During his time teaching, Clinton worked on many political campaigns. He considered himself a Democrat and supported George McGovern's presidential bid in 1972. McGovern lost to President Nixon.

A few years later, Clinton decided the time was right for him to run for political office. In 1974, he entered the race for a seat in the U.S. House of Representatives. Hillary joined him in Arkansas to help his campaign. He lost the election, but on October 11, 1975, Clinton and Hillary were married. They continued to teach together at the university.

Clinton's career in politics began in earnest when he was elected Arkansas' attorney general, the state's chief lawyer. Hillary worked as a lawyer as well. They moved to the capital city of Little Rock. As attorney general, Clinton met influential people and began

> **"There is nothing wrong in America that can't be fixed with what is right in America."**
> *Bill Clinton*

shaping his ideas on conserving energy and protecting the environment.

By 1978, Clinton was ready for bigger things. He ran for governor, promising to improve Arkansas' school systems, which were among the worst in the country. Following his victory, he worked on health care and energy issues. Clinton lost popularity by raising gas taxes and allowing President Carter to re-locate Cuban refugees to the state. Some of these displaced Cubans caused a riot at Fort Chaffee. In 1980, Clinton lost his re-election for governor. It was a low point in his political career.

Clinton received a Rhodes scholarship to study at Oxford University.

Clinton's Political Career

"As times change, so government must change. We need a new government for a new century, humble enough not to try to solve all our problems for us, but strong enough to give us the tools to solve our problems for ourselves; a government that is smaller, lives within its means, and does more with less." *Bill Clinton*

Clinton did not give up after his loss in the 1980 election. He traveled around the state, giving speeches to gain people's respect. He earned the nickname "The Comeback Kid" by winning the election for the governor's office in 1982. Clinton was re-elected in 1984 and 1986. His successes in Arkansas earned him national recognition.

In 1992, Clinton accepted the Democratic nomination for president. During his campaign against incumbent President George Bush, rumors circulated about Clinton's character. People said he had been unfaithful to his wife. Hillary, however, stood by him, and he won the election.

As president, Clinton worked to compromise with the Republican-controlled Congress. He pursued his goal of balancing the federal budget. He worked for the passage of a bill that required background checks on anyone wanting to purchase a gun. Clinton enacted the Family and Medical Leave Act, which allowed employees to take time away from

Bill Clinton, with his wife Hillary, spoke at the National Governor's Association in 1987.

work if they were seriously ill or needed to take care of a newborn child.

Clinton's many successes helped him win re-election in 1996. However, several personal issues would threaten his presidency. Clinton and Hillary were investigated as the result of a land deal that some believed was illegal. He was sued by Paula Jones, a former Arkansas state employee. She said Clinton had dealt with her inappropriately. Investigators uncovered evidence that he may have lied under oath about rumors that he had had an affair with White House intern Monica Lewinsky. The U.S. House of Representatives decided there was enough evidence to impeach President Clinton and sent the case to the Senate for a trial. Clinton was found not guilty, and he remained popular until the end of his second term.

Meanwhile, Clinton worked on several peace agreements between Israel and its neighbors. He signed a bill to balance the federal budget, and he ordered U.S. forces into the Kosovo region of Serbia to prevent Serbians from killing Albanians who lived there. Clinton worked on laws to help further protect the environment. By the end of his second term in office, the economy was booming, and unemployment was at a 30-year low.

In early 2001, Clinton left office. After his term ended, the Clintons moved to Chappaqua, New York. Clinton then began helping his wife with her own political ambitions. In 2000, Hillary was elected to the U.S. Senate in New York.

In 2007, Hillary Rodham Clinton began her campaign to become the first female president of the United States.

HILLARY RODHAM CLINTON

Hillary Rodham Clinton took her role as First Lady seriously. Like Eleanor Roosevelt and Rosalynn Carter, Hillary stood by her husband and helped him make important political decisions. She was an active participant in his campaigns. She gave speeches, offered advice, and even served on a committee that was in charge of creating a national health care plan.

Hillary has been a lawyer, author, law professor, mother, child advocate, public policy expert, and most recently, a U.S. Senator for the state of New York. Like her husband, she has always been interested in politics and felt strongly about women's roles in them. In 2007, Hillary announced her intentions to run for president. She is trying to become the first woman to win her party's nomination for president.

Impeachment

When the Founding Fathers first wrote the Constitution, they had to think about the problems that might come up in running the country. They realized that at some time a president might commit a crime while in office. The Constitution gives Congress the power to impeach the president to remove him or her from office.

"If you live long enough, you'll make mistakes. But if you learn from them, you'll be a better person. It's how you handle adversity, not how it affects you. The main thing is never quit, never quit, never quit." *Bill Clinton*

The impeachment process starts in the U.S. House of Representatives. A majority of its members must agree that they believe the president has committed a crime. They then vote to impeach the president, and the action moves to the U.S. Senate. The Senate is responsible for carrying out a trial against the president. Senators hear testimony and collect evidence to try to prove whether a crime was actually committed. The president is allowed to enlist lawyers to defend him and to explain his actions. The trial concludes with a vote by the Senate. A two-thirds majority is required to remove the president. Otherwise, the president is acquitted and allowed to remain in office.

BREAKING NEWS
President Clinton's Grand
Jury Testimony

CNN

President Bill Clinton had to testify before a grand jury about his conduct with White House intern Monica Lewinsky.

Clinton had been under investigation near the end of his first term for his role in an improper investment in a land deal. That trial was known as the Whitewater Scandal. It was during that trial that another problem surfaced for Clinton. A woman who had worked in the Arkansas government while he was governor claimed Clinton had treated her inappropriately. She planned to sue the president for his actions. It was during this time that rumors began circulating that President Clinton had been involved in an affair with a young intern who worked in the White House.

During the trial, President Clinton denied any involvement with either woman. A lawyer named Kenneth Starr was assigned to investigate the charges and discovered evidence that he believed proved Clinton had lied while under oath. Lying under oath, called perjury, is a crime. Starr charged that Clinton committed a crime by lying while giving testimony.

In 1998, the House of Representatives conducted impeachment proceedings based on Starr's charges. A majority vote in the House meant Clinton would go to trial in the Senate to face

charges of perjury. Some Americans questioned whether Clinton should be on trial. They agreed he had acted inappropriately, but felt it was part of his personal life and did not affect his ability to run the country. Others felt that he had lied in court and should be punished even if it meant removing him from office. The proceedings caused tension between Democrats and Republicans.

In 1999, the Senate concluded the trial and voted to acquit Clinton. He was found not guilty of any crimes and was allowed to remain in office. While many Americans felt Clinton was not honest, he remained a popular president until the end of his second term because of his successful political policies.

The U.S. House of Representatives has voted to impeach only two presidents. They were Andrew Johnson in 1867 and Bill Clinton in 1998. Both were acquitted of their crimes during a Senate trial.

Kenneth Starr addressed the House of Representatives about impeaching President Clinton.

George W. Bush's Early Years

George Walker Bush was born in New Haven, Connecticut, on July 6, 1946. His parents came from wealthy East Coast families. Politics played a large part in the Bush family. George's great-grandfather was a close advisor to Vice President Hubert Humphrey. His grandfather was a U.S. Senator, and his father became president. George's future in politics seemed guaranteed.

After his family moved to Houston, Texas, George was sent to the same private school his father had attended, Phillips Academy. Following in his father's footsteps was a challenge. George's father had been a popular student who excelled both in the classroom and on the baseball diamond. George followed his father by attending Yale.

During the late 1960s, many young people were being drafted to fight in the Vietnam War. Bush joined the Texas Air National Guard, a reserve military unit. He flew airplanes for them on weekends over the next six years.

Bush earned a master's degree in business administration from Harvard and then headed back to his childhood home in Midland, Texas. He began a career in the oil business. He met Laura Welch,

a school librarian, through a mutual friend. After a whirlwind three-month courtship, the couple married on November 5, 1977. The next year, Bush made a brief attempt at politics. He ran for a seat in Congress and lost.

Throughout his time in school and in the National Guard, Bush helped his father campaign. He realized he liked

George W. Bush (right) is not the only Bush son to follow his father into a political career. Brother Jeb (left) became governor of Florida.

life on the campaign trail. Bush was at his father's side when he became vice president in 1980 and then president in 1988. The public exposure allowed Bush to secure a group of investors to purchase the Texas Rangers baseball franchise. Bush had always loved baseball. He managed the business side of the team and helped secure a new stadium. Later, he would sell the team and make millions from his investment.

Around the time his father lost his bid for re-election, Bush was again ready to enter the political arena. He ran for governor of Texas against a much-loved grandmother named Ann Richards. Richards underestimated Bush as an opponent. Bush felt that, if he concentrated on some key issues, including reducing crime, improving education, and reforming welfare, he might have a chance at victory. He was right. He won the governor's office in 1994.

> "I believe the most solemn duty of the American president is to protect the American people. If America shows uncertainty and weakness in this decade, the world will drift toward tragedy. This will not happen on my watch." *George W. Bush*

Bush brought new ideas to government. He had specific ideas about the role government should play. Bush described himself as a "compassionate" conservative who felt states and cities should assume a greater role in governing the people. He believed in strong family values and taking personal responsibility for one's actions.

As governor, Bush set out to make positive changes in Texas. He worked to improve the state's schools, to enforce the death penalty, and to reform the state's welfare system. He was re-elected to a second term in 1998. In 2000, Bush felt it was time to follow in his father's footsteps one more time. He ran for president.

George W. Bush led an ownership group that controlled the Texas Rangers baseball team before becoming the state's governor.

Bush's Presidency

> "Recognizing and confronting our history is important. Transcending our history is essential. We are not limited by what we have done, or what we have left undone. We are limited only by what we are willing to do."
>
> *George W. Bush*

The 2000 election was between Bush and President Clinton's vice president, Al Gore. While Gore was in office, the economy was strong. Unemployment and inflation were at all-time lows, but many Americans liked Bush's conservative views on family and government.

Early on, it looked like Gore might win. He had more popular votes than Bush. He had a lead, with 267 electoral votes to Bush's 245. However, Florida and its 25 electoral votes would decide the election.

After Bush was named the victor, errors were discovered in the vote count. A controversy surrounded the election, and eventually, the U.S. Supreme Court stepped in and declared Bush the winner. Gore had won the popular vote, but Bush received more electoral votes. It was only the third time in U.S. history that the candidate with the most popular votes lost the election.

During his first term in office, Bush worked on domestic issues. He decreased taxes and created a new health care plan for senior citizens. His education reform called "No Child Left Behind" made states and schools accountable for the success of their students and gave parents flexibility in choosing which schools their children attended.

George W. Bush served as president during the September 11, 2001, terrorist attacks.

On September 11, 2001, a disastrous event occurred that would dominate Bush's focus for the rest of his time in office. Terrorists attacked New York and Washington, D.C. They flew planes into the World Trade Center and the Pentagon. Bush now had a new mission. It was to fight global terrorism. He quickly created the Department of Homeland Security and passed the Patriot Act to increase information sharing between intelligence-gathering agencies, such as the Federal Bureau of Investigation and the Central Intelligence Agency.

The terrorist group al-Qaeda claimed responsibility for the attacks. Its leader, Osama Bin Laden, was in the Taliban-controlled area of Afghanistan. Bush tried to negotiate with the Taliban government for Bin Laden's surrender. When his request was denied, Bush launched an attack and removed the Taliban from power.

Bush then worked to convince the United Nations Security Council that Saddam Hussein needed to be removed from power in Iraq. Bush believed Hussein had stockpiled weapons of mass destruction, such as chemical and biological weapons. American forces, with British and Australian troops, invaded Iraq. In just a few short weeks, they took control of the capital city of Baghdad.

During this time, Bush pressed forward with his campaign to win re-election in 2004. He defeated Democratic Senator John Kerry of Massachusetts, winning both the popular vote and the electoral vote.

Stabilizing Iraq proved a much greater task than Bush had thought. Even after Saddam Hussein was removed from power, various factions continued attacking U.S. troops stationed there. America's military victory was turning into a long, drawn-out siege with no foreseeable end. Support for the war began to erode as the cost of the war rose and more lives were lost.

MIDDLE EAST MAP

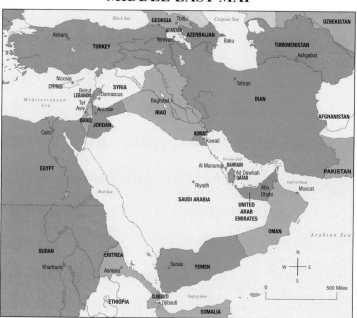

THE IRAQ WAR

The Iraq War began in 2003 with the U.S.-led invasion of Iraq. A coalition of forces overthrew the government led by Saddam Hussein and occupied Iraq. The United States hoped to help the people of Iraq establish a stable and democratic government. Despite its efforts, the coalition was unable to restore order to the country. Various **insurgent** groups continued to fight and resorted to acts of terrorism. The main cultural groups in Iraq, Kurds, Sunni Muslims, and Shia Muslims, argued over who should control the government and country. World leaders feared Iraq was headed toward a civil war.

The war remains a controversial issue for America. Its outcome and the future of Iraq are still in doubt.

Timeline

The contemporary era began with a conflict in Vietnam and the Cold War. However, the presidents of the time managed to successfully lead the country forward, despite scandals and economic struggles.

1950s	**1960s**	**1970s**
PRESIDENTS		
In 1952, Dwight Eisenhower is elected as the 34th president of the United States. Richard Nixon serves as his vice president. 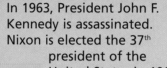	In 1963, President John F. Kennedy is assassinated. Nixon is elected the 37th president of the United States in 1968.	In 1973, Vice President Spiro Agnew resigns because of bribery charges. A year later, President Nixon resigns because of the Watergate Scandal.
UNITED STATES		
In 1959, the first U.S. military advisors are sent to South Vietnam to help it defend itself against communist North Vietnam.	Martin Luther King, Jr. is assassinated in 1968 as civil rights tensions rise.	In 1973, the last U.S. troops in Vietnam return home. Shortly after, North Vietnam takes over South Vietnam.
WORLD		
North Korean forces invade South Korea in 1950. This action leads to the Korean War, during which the United States helps South Korea defend itself from communist North Korea.	*Apollo 11* lands on the Moon, and astronaut Neil Armstrong becomes the first person to walk on the Moon.	In 1979, Russia invades Afghanistan. That same year, Iranian students take a group of U.S. citizens hostage.

Today, terrorism, not communism, is the leading cause of concern. It has yet to be determined whether future presidents will be able to successfully lead the country forward through this new struggle as presidents during the Cold War were able to do in the past.

1980s	1990s	2000s
PRESIDENTS		
Ronald Reagan is elected as the 40th president of the United States, and George Bush is his vice president. The U.S. hostages in Iran are released shortly after Reagan wins the election.	Bill Clinton is elected as the 42nd president of the United States in 1992. He is re-elected in 1996.	In 2000, George W. Bush is elected as the 43rd president of the United States. He wins re-election in 2004.
UNITED STATES		
In 1986, the Space Shuttle *Challenger* explodes.	President Clinton faces impeachment, but is eventually found not guilty of any wrongdoing. 	In 2001, terrorists attack the World Trade Center in New York City and the Pentagon in Washington, D.C. Bush declares a war on terrorism and leads a coalition to remove the Taliban government from power in Afghanistan.
WORLD		
In 1989, the Berlin Wall comes down. East and West Germany are united shortly after. 	The Persian Gulf War begins in 1991 after Iraq invades neighboring Kuwait.	The Iraq War begins in 2003. Iraqi forces are defeated, and Saddam Hussein is removed from power. As the United States continues its occupation of Iraq and Iraqi insurgents attack U.S. troops, the war becomes increasingly unpopular.

Activity

Balancing the federal budget has been a struggle for U.S. presidents since the birth of the United States. Early on, the U.S. government had to borrow money for wars it had been in. Today, the government continues to borrow money to support itself. Try creating your own budget.

Begin by listing any income you earn. The government gets most of its money through taxes, but you may earn an allowance or do chores. You may earn money by baby-sitting or mowing neighbors' yards. Add this all up to determine how much money you will make in a year.

Next, list the cost of all of the things that you will need throughout the year. The government needs to spend money on defense and social programs to help its citizens. You may need to spend money on lunch or to buy gas for the lawn mower you use to mow neighbors' yards. Total the cost of your "needs."

Write a list of the cost of your "wants." These things are not necessary. They are things you would like to have or do. You may want to buy a video game or go to a movie. Total the cost of your wants.

Add the total of your "needs" and "wants," and then subtract this sum from your income. If you have money left over, you have a surplus. If you do not have enough money to cover the cost of your needs and wants, you have a deficit.

Lastly, balance your budget. If you have a surplus, you could either save the extra money for the future or spend it on other wants this year. If you have a deficit, you will either need to find a source of more income or cut spending. The government usually raises taxes or borrows money when it has a deficit, or it cuts spending on programs it does not feel are important. You will need to choose if you want to borrow money, work more, or cut spending. Remember, if you borrow money, you will need to find a way to pay it back. If you cut spending, you can only cut spending from your "wants."

Quiz

1. True or False? Richard Nixon was the first president to visit the Soviet Union.

2. Which president received offers to play professional football with the Green Bay Packers and the Detroit Lions?
A. Gerald Ford
B. Jimmy Carter
C. Bill Clinton

3. True or False? Jimmy Carter's family owned and ran a peanut farm.

4. Which president played a saxophone with a jazz band named The Three Blind Mice?
A. Jimmy Carter
B. Bill Clinton
C. George W. Bush

5. True or False? George W. Bush was rescued by a submarine during World War II.

6. Who led the country in Operation Desert Storm against Iraq after it invaded the small country of Kuwait?
A. George H.W. Bush
B. Bill Clinton
C. George W. Bush

7. Who was president of the United States on September 11, 2001, when terrorists flew planes into the World Trade Center and the Pentagon?
A. Ronald Reagan
B. Bill Clinton
C. George W. Bush

8. True or False? Ronald Reagan was assassinated during his term as president.

9. Which president was the first in the history of the United States to resign from office?
A. Richard Nixon
B. Bill Clinton
C. George W. Bush

Answers 1. True 2. A 3. False 4. B 5. False. His father, George H. W. Bush, was rescued by a submarine in World War II. 6. A 7. C 8. False. There was an assassination attempt on Reagan's life, but he recovered from his wound. 9. A

Further Research

Books

To find out more about U.S. presidents, visit your local library. Most libraries have computers that connect to a database for researching information. If you enter a keyword, you will be provided with a list of books in the library that contain information on that topic. Non-fiction books are arranged numerically, using their call number. Fiction books are organized alphabetically by the author's last name.

Websites

The World Wide Web is also a good source of information. Reputable websites usually include government sites, educational sites, and online encyclopedias. Visit the following sites to learn more about U.S. presidents.

The official White House website offers a short history of the U.S. presidency, along with biographical sketches and portraits of all the presidents to date. **www.whitehouse.gov/history/presidents**

This website contains background information, election results, cabinet members, and notable events for each of the presidents. **www.ipl.org/div/potus**

Explore the lives and careers of every U.S. president on the PBS website. **www.pbs.org/wgbh/amex/presidents**

Glossary

assassination: to kill someone, most often an important person, such as a world leader

campaign: to actively seek a political office through giving speeches or attending rallies

coalition: an alliance or group of people or countries, which come together for a common cause

communism: a form of government in which the central government holds all the power, not the people of the country

deficit: excessive of spending when compared to income

democracy: a form of government that is ruled by the people; officials are elected to office by the people

economy: the way a country earns and spends its money

hostage: a person who is held prisoner by a group or government; a hostage is usually held for political reasons

impeached: removed a president from office

inauguration: the ceremony that is carried out when a new president begins his or her term

incumbent: a person who holds an office or post

inflation: a sharp rise or sudden increase in the price of goods and services

insurgent: a member of a political party or group that rebels against the government

negotiations: discussions about a situation or issue in order to reach an agreement

nomination: when a political party chooses someone to represent them in a political campaign and election

Quaker: a member of a religious group that is dedicated to peaceful principles

segregation: the act of separating groups of people based on race, religion, or gender

Index